# For My People

A Book of Poetry and Short Stories by
*Anthony Arnold*

# My People,

# Our Trials and Tribulations

*By Anthony Arnold*

Steamy Trails Publishing

ISBN-13: 978-0985118525 (Steamy Trails Publishing)
ISBN-10: 0985118520

LCCN: 2012938271

www.steamytrailspublishing.com

PRINTED IN THE UNITED STATES of AMERICA

I dedicate this book to the 3 women who made me who I am
My Great-grandmother, Maggie Nelson
My grandmother, Evelyn Livingston
My Mother, Marolyn Martin
Without you I am nothing
Love you!

# Contents

# Acknowledgements

Honoring the most high is a must, first and foremost. The very possibility of this book is truly by the grace of God. I wholeheartedly thank him for my talent.

To my mom for having me and to my wonderful children; daughter, Jordan and son, Anthony. Love you guys with all my heart!

A special thanks to my inspiration and muse, Rosemarie Howard. Thank you for all the love, encouragement and unwavering support you have given me to make this happen…love you babe!

God has blessed me with the most supportive people from the very moment I began writing:
Lynnie Rose, RoseApples, BlaqueRose, Cheryl, Silva, Lora, Latrice, Rosalind Cherry, Jen Jen, Wingman, Kenneth, Jon, Wayne, Rodney and Kevin who have all become my poetic family. I appreciate you all greatly.

A special thanks to Nyla, my favorite BTR host, thank you for allowing me to be heard.

To Nita and Katrina of Steamy Trails Publishing
for providing the platform to display my talent.

Finally to all my other poetic brethren, thank you for your love, support, criticism and suggestions. It has made me a better writer and a better person.

Thanks to you all for going on this journey with me!

*Grasshopper humbly bows!*
*Anthony*

# Introduction

I have always been a student of black history and since I grew up in the 60's, have always been fascinated with the civil rights movement. So it only made sense that when I started writing again that I would focus on this.

For us as a people, slavery is the beginning. Without this event in our history, we do not exist. One of my stories, *"My Journey-My story"*, deals with a young slave from the time of his capture until his settlement on a plantation and his almost death on that same plantation. This is one of my favorite pieces because it shows the perseverance and the faith that our people had to overcome and everything placed in front of them!

I hope that when you read this, it will give you a taste of what they went through. The blood, sweat and tears that were shed so that we are able to express ourselves in this fashion. I hope that it will make you think, wonder, and sometimes cry for those who were here before us.

I came up with the title, *"My People, Our Trials and Tribulations"*, as a tribute to the fortitude, the courage and the strength of our ancestors as they fought and sometimes died to make themselves seen as a people.

This was a labor of love. I hear them speak to me, and after reading the poems and short stories within this book, I hope you do as well!

## Ancestors whispers...

*"I see my people struggle"*

# My People, Our Trials And Tribulations

## <u>My People</u>

I hear the voices of the ancestors whisper
Who are you? What have you done?
I see my people struggle and try to survive
Young people with no purpose
No idea from whence they came

They don't know that they are descended from
Royalty, Rulers of Mesopotamia and Egypt
Pharaohs and Kings
They don't know

They don't know the things that we went through
So that they can walk around with pants sagging,
Music blaring, drugs dealing, black on black killing
They don't know

It hurts me to see where we are
The things that we haven't done
We have not progressed
We have regressed

It brings me to tears to watch my people suffer
That's why I speak like I do, teach like I do,
Write what I do, give the way I do
Because I do know

The ancestors speak through me
Teach through me, help through me
And I will continue anyway I can

**I am a proud black man!**

# Slavery

Brought over from a far off land
Families ripped apart
Men, women, and children
Generations decimated

Carried in ships across the sea
Packed inside like cattle
Some might make it, some might not
Death is a companion, bodies left to rot

Bought and sold like common sheep
Teeth examined, breasts squeezed
Branded and numbered
Not a person, property

Running to escape trying to get away
Slave hunters on the prowl
Beaten, maimed, killed outright
Drag them home an example to make

The War between the States
Trying to protect a way of life
North against south
Freedom versus slavery

The emancipation proclamation
Freedom to the slaves
No place to go
Slaves to a new day

## <u>Slave Ship</u>

I am a slave ship
The things that I have seen
and heard I am not proud of
Yet I must do my master's will

I am only a vessel of wood and linen
I have no soul, no feelings
For if I did I would truly be ashamed
I could only do my master's will

My keel was laid in the late 1500
I was designed to carry 400 slaves
and if need be I could carry 500
All to satisfy the need for slaves

Laid head to foot,
I carried my cargo across the oceans,
through fair weather or foul
Not all of them made it, but it was not my place to care
I could only do my master's will

I heard the cries and the prayers of those inside my walls
Why have you forsaken me?
Where is my wife? My children?
I could not answer them, I could not help them,
could not soothe them
I could only do my master's will

Great sickness swept through my decks, many died
Thrown overboard as if they didn't exist
Just more room to place more
I am just an object, yet I wanted to cry but could not

Coming in to port, my cargo unloaded
Stay just long to replenish my goods
and to repair or replace what was needed
Off again to do my master's will

I made many trips across the great water
Transporting many generations of families
Watching many more come to a watery end
Doing my master's will

My time finally came to an end in 1867
I was wrecked in a storm carrying 523 souls
A relief swept through my timbers
As I settled to my watery grave

I no longer had to listen to the screams
Feel the agony, and the pain
I no longer had to watch the bodies thrown away
I no longer had to do my master's will

## A Slave's Prayer

Father I raise my eyes to thee
What have I done to have this on me?
Taken away from my home
My family no more to see

Placed aboard this floating terror
Freedom taken away
Mashed in like cattle
We are no longer men

Death and discomfort follow us across the sea
Some of us the end never to see
Father why have you forsaken us
Why have you taken away your trust?

I pray to you please let me die
no longer can I live, no more can I try
I know not what is on the other end
I cannot see what is around the bend

Deliver me from my trespassers
Let me come home to you
My lord, do for me what is best
Let me come home to rest

**Amen**

# My journey-My story

My name is Adebayo and this is my story.

I was the first-born to my Oba and Iya, living in a small tribe in Nigeria. My name, which means, *"He came in a joyful time"*, showed the prosperity of my tribe and family.

As a tribal elder, my father was greatly blessed with his first born being a son. Our linage would be ensured…Our family would be continued. Little did we know what the future would hold and that none of that would matter.

As a ruler's first born this meant that my mate would be arranged for me. As I was to follow rite of passage and follow my father as ruler of our tribe. I was groomed to be a future chief; I was shown the way of men. Even as a small child, I was taken under the elders care.

On the sunrise of my sixth year my Iya had another child named, Abiola, *"Born in honor"*. Our family was truly blessed.

I grew tall and strong, I was fastest among boys my age and could track any animal.
My education was almost complete.

On the sunrise of my fourteenth year, I underwent the manhood ceremony. I was circumcised and smoked the
ceremonial plant. During this time it is said visions shall be seen. I saw myself going far away from my home. I did not know how right this would prove to be.

At the time of my ceremony, I was introduced to my mate.
Her name was Abisola, meaning *"born into a wealthy family"*. She was the daughter of a chief of a neighboring tribe. This ensured that we were family, that the two tribes would be protected.

Or so we thought.

Before the sun rose, screams set forth, I ran from our tent to see pale men with fire sticks in our village making a loud noise. My father led the warriors and elders to protect our homes but their spears and bows were no match for the fire sticks and they were all killed.

The pale men captured me and others my age and placed us in chains while they gathered the women and proceeded to rape and kill most of them. I heard Abisola scream as three pale men took her into our tent. I heard her call my name, *"Adebayo! Adebayo!"*

And then silence.

I thrashed like a wild man trying to help my mate.
Two of the pale men fought to hold me down, then a third one hit me on my head.

Blackness.

When I awoke even though it felt like I had been out for days, it was only hours. My village was gone, my family was gone, my life was gone.

We were chained together and began the march to the big water.
We were marched day and night to the big water.
Some of us died, and left where they fell.

Why had our gods forsaken us?
We marched for 5 cycles of the sun, given little water or food I listened to the cries of the ones taken wondering why.

Why?

On the cycle of the sixth day we arrived at our destination.

It was bigger than any boat that I had ever seen and we were not
the only ones to be put upon this ship.
There were many of us standing, waiting.

These men loaded us upon this ship, laying head to foot,
packed in close as they could put us, stilled chained.
Barely able to turn, nowhere to go darkness everywhere.
Crying, praying, and wondering where would we end?

Everyday someone dies. They stopped having the will to live. This
would give us more room but you never knew who was next. They
threw salt water on us to try and keep us clean but it burned as the
salt got into the wounds from the chains.

They fed us just enough to keep us alive. Food that I would not
have given the animals in my village. They had to keep us alive,
but for what was the question. They argued and fought amongst
themselves about us. Some wanted to dump us into the big water,
others said we should be left at the nearest island. But we
continued on.

Half way through the journey, a great sickness came upon us, and a
lot of us died. The men brought us to the top deck where the sun
was so bright that I could not see. Finally as I could, all I could see
was water everywhere. My gods had forsaken me and I was truly
going to die.

We traveled for many cycles of the sun and I could not keep count
any more. I watched as they threw those who had died overboard,
and the waters ran red with their blood as they were eaten. I did not
pray any more as I felt that I had been forsaken by my god. I
existed by my own will, I refused to die. I would not.

One morning I felt the ship slow and we were not brought upon the
deck. I could tell there was a change in the crewmen. They seemed

happier and moved with a purpose. I heard one say, "*Finally this is over and we can get these darkies off of my ship*".

We were chained and taken out of the hole that had been our home for so long. There were many of these pale people here. They were everywhere. I was to learn that they were called whites. I looked around and saw those of my color walking around, but when I looked at them they either would not look at me or would look at me as I were the devil.

Where am I and what is going to become of me?

We were taken to this pin where we were looked at; teeth, arms, and legs. Even our private parts were looked at. One white said he will breed well; he is hung like a horse!
This person took me and five more of us and marched up to a big dark person and said get them to the plantation, clean them up and get them clothed. I want them ready to go in the field in the morning.

The slave looked at us and said, "*I know you don't understand me, but you are now the property of Mr. Tom Jones. He is fair, but he can be mean as well. As long as you know your place you will be ok. If you try to escape life will not be good and you will die.*
*My name is Jackson and I was once like you. Scared and didn't know what to do. Mr. Tom made me the slave overseer and I answer to only him. I have no feelings for you and I will do what he tells me. If that means that I have to maim or kill one of you I will. Let's go we have a long way to go and a lot to do.*"

We were taken to this big house and went to a place that would be known as the hill. This is where I would live the next 20 years of my life. We were taken out of the wagon and went to the yard where Jackson told us to take off our clothes. When we did not move fast enough, he went to one and ripped off his clothing and told us to do the same. Women came and brought water and soap and began to scrub us. They made comments about our privates and went through our hair looking for lice. After about twenty minutes of this we were given shirts and pants and told to dress. We were then taken to the barn and told this would be where we would sleep tonight. We were also given a stew and bread. This was better than anything we had on the ship, but my stomach could not hold it. Then I heard a voice. It sounded like my Abisola, but it could not be. She was gone. This vision said to me, my name is Marie, and you must eat slowly. She brought me more and made sure that I took my time. After that I fell into a fitful slumber.

I was assigned to work in the fields as a field hand. This I did not mind because I was able to see Marie as she brought water to us. She helped me to learn the language and help make myself understood. I began to tell her of my home and what happened to my brother and my family. She shook her head and the tears ran down her face as I told her what had happened to Abisola. She kissed me on my cheek and walked away. I still thought about my family, but it seemed less and less. When I tried to see Abisola's face all I could see was Marie. I took it as a sign from the gods as this would be my destiny.

One day though some thing happened that would change everything that I thought could be. Mr. Tom Jones and Mr. Jackson came and got me from the fields.

*"Tie him to the tree."* Mr. Jones said.

I could not understand what was going on and I asked, *"What did I do? What did I do?"*

*Did you go into my house and steal from me?*

I said, *"No boss I have never been to the big house."*

*Do not lie to me, did you steal from me?*

*"No boss! No boss!",* I said.

10 lashes. Jackson looked at me as he uncoiled the whip. I heard the pop as he began to limber up his arm.

*"Tell the truth and I will go easy on you."*

*"I never been to the big house."*

I heard the whip snap and felt a searing pain as it cut into my back. I screamed as it cut into my flesh.

*"Tell me the truth."* Jackson said.

*"No boss, I didn't do it!"*

Once again the whip cut into my flesh, and again I screamed, *"No boss, no boss, I didn't do it!"*
After 3 more lashes, Jackson turned to Mr. Jones and said, *"I believe him. I can make any one confess with this here whip, not him."*

Jones said, *"Cut him down and take care of his wounds, don't need to get them infected."*

I was brought back to the barn so Marie could take care of my wounds. She gasped when she saw me. She went a got warm water to cleanse the blood off my back and then proceeded to put horse liniment into the wounds and bandaged my back. I was barely aware of this and the kiss that she gave me as she sat with me for what would turn out to be three days.

I awoke with a start. I thought that I was still in Africa, yet I was still in this strange land call America. After my beating, I decided that I had to get away from here. I saw what happened to slaves who tried to escape. They were either beaten or killed but I knew I could make it. I didn't tell Marie because I did not want her to be harmed. But I knew I must leave here or die trying.

I waited a week. I saved food to carry with me. I was as ready as I was going to be. Late one night when there was no moon, I snuck away from the barn with my little package of food. I ran through the forest. I could always run, so I thought I could put a good distance away from the plantation.

I had been on the run for two days when I ran into them. The slave hunters. The dogs had picked up my scent and had been tracking me and now I was caught. They tied me to the back of a wagon and took me back to the farm.

Mr. Jones paid the hunters and told Jackson to pick four strong slaves and to bring me to the big tree in the yard and to bring every one so that they could see. The four other slaves held me while Jackson tied my arms and legs to the tree.

Mr. Jones took the whip from Jackson and said, *"This is what happens when you run away from me."*

I heard the swish of the whip and felt the pain as it tore into the wounds that were already on my back. I could feel the blood flow and the tears ran down my face. Again and again it continued, until even Jackson could not stand any more.

*"Boss you gonna kill him."*

Jones looked at him and said, *"Do you want to be in his place?"* Jackson turned away, disgusted.

Finally he finished and when they went to untie me he said, *"Leave him there! If he is alive in the morning then cut him down."*

I felt a cool cloth on my face. It was Marie. I watched the tears fall down her face and made up my mind that I would not die, that I would live, that I would survive.

I did survive and I did live. Over the next fourteen years I loved again. I married Marie and had children. I lived to see all of us become free, because of something called the emancipation proclamation. As I watch my own children grow I see my Oba, Iya and my brother. I also see Abisola in my Marie's eyes. I passed on my journey to my children and hope that they pass it on to their children and their children's children...The journey of a man from a small village in Nigeria, who survived anguish, heartbreak and despair, to come to a new world and survive.

## Chains

Chains have imprisoned our people for centuries
From ancient times, when we turned our back on our own
Separating father from son,
mother from daughter,
husband from wife
Locked liked animals in a zoo and
paraded thru bush and jungle
Dragged if need be

Chains allowed us to be taken from our ancestral homes
Locked to the bottom of a ship
Never to see our homes again
Never to see our land again

Chains help to sell us, to hold us, to beat us
And sometimes to kill us
To maim us, to rape us, and to sell us

Today we are still held by chains, we just can't see them
Chains of racism, money, drugs, jealousy of each other
It is up to us to break these chains that hold us down
Keep us under and break us apart

**I've shed mine, will you?**

## Chains pt 2

You may have me chained
but you can't keep me down
My soul will fly
My heart will beat on

My body may be bloodied
but my head is unbowed
I am beaten but not cowed
I am a proud black man

Shackles may hold me still
but my mind will fly
You cannot stop me
No matter how hard you try

These chains cannot hold
who I am or what I am
If I perish others will take my place
You cannot stop what you don't understand

So try your best to break me down
to crush my spirit
These chains cannot hold me

**I am a king**

## Haiku

Chains bind us tightly
Slowly we walk
Never seeing home again

=====

March for justice
Dogs and police strike
Death follows

=====

I am a king
Royal blood flows through my veins
I am just a slave

=====

Running for my life
Hear the dogs barking
I am at an end

=====

Separate entrance, can't sit here
No coloreds allowed
Sit-in's happening

=====

Ropes hang from trees
2 men swinging
Lives ended too soon

=====

A hotel in Memphis
A shot booms
A dream silenced

=====

A march in Washington
200,000 strong
I have a dream

=====

A theater stage speaking
An X killed
By any means necessary
=====

The Underground Railroad
A means to an end
Freedom!
=====

People bought and sold
Family's ripped apart
Slavery endures
=====

Escape for freedom
Caught, beaten, maimed
Six feet underground
=====

Martin and Malcolm
A dream by any means necessary
Silenced forever
=====

A transit bus
A black woman and a white man
History is changed…forever
=====

The gospel train is comin
The Underground Railroad is here
Freedom abounds

## <u>A Dream</u>

Dr. King said he had a dream
but how close are we to achieving that dream?
We complain about the treatment we receive from others
But as it was written,
*" let he who is without sin cast the first stone"*

We as a people are our own worst enemy
Instead of helping each other, we try to bring each other down
Instead of building up, we want to tear down
Instead of trying to be a role model for our kids,
we let them worship the athlete, the entertainer,
and yes the drug dealer

Some don't remember the riots in
Detroit, in Watts, and even in Liberty City
but I do
Some don't remember the Klan riding around with sheets on
but I do
Some have never seen the signs
"nigger don't let the sun go down on your ass in this town",
but I have

We have to get over this petty treatment of each other
and learn to help ourselves as a people
If not I fear we will be right back to those days
When Dr. King said, *"I have a dream"*

# By Any Means Necessary

By any means necessary was the battle cry
We were tired and to stop this we must try
40 acres and a mule was their answer to our call
What they didn't know was we planned to make them fall

They beat, shot and hung, intending to make a fuss
But that ended when Miss Rosa said,
*"I'm not sitting in the back of no bus!"*
They hung Emmitt Till, for something you do with your eye
Because he had the boldness to look at a white woman as she
walked by

They killed Medgar Evers in the driveway of his home,
so long ago it must seem
They shot Martin Luther king, because he said,
*"I have a dream"*
They even killed their own kind,
because they raised their voices to sing
They killed the brothers Kennedy,
because they wanted to let freedom ring

I sit back and wonder how they would feel today
To see how everything has gone, how thing are in disarray
Who do we follow, who will pick up the fight
These are the things we must do, because it is our right

We must help ourselves, we must stay wary
We must move on…

**BY ANY MEANS NECESSARY!!!!!!!**

# Freedom

Riding on this bus to help our own
Freedom is what we seek; life is what we want grown
The courts say you can't keep us out
We are gonna prove this to use our new found clout

We should have known bigotry recognizes no court
And racism for some is just a sport
To kill for some to uphold Jim Crow
This is their way of life
No uppity niggas are going to stop what they know

On May 14, 1961 on a day to salute your mother
The Klan tried to kill us all; wife, husband, sister, and brother
They firebombed our bus, held the doors to keep us in
To burn us all even though it was a sin

By the grace of god we got out alive
We were more determined, to succeed we did strive
We did not stop, we continued on the bus
Even though we were condemned by the president
As unpatriotic and continuing to raise a fuss

We were beaten with pipes, bats, and chains
Incarcerated in jails and prisons
But we held fast to our beliefs
For freedom was our reason

I survived those days; my life went by so fast
And I would do it all again
To ensure injustice wouldn't last

In my golden age
I raise my voice to sing,

*"FREE AT LAST, FREE AT LAST*
*THANK GOD ALMIGHTY*
*IM FREE AT LAST!"*

------------

This is dedicated to the brave men and women
Who risked their lives to ensure our way of life.
God bless you all!

## <u>Clouds</u>

I look into the clouds
I can see the faces of my forbearers
As they gaze upon me
As they speak to me

I hear their voices in the wind
I feel their love in the warmth of the sun
I can see their passion in the lightning
And feel their anguish in the thunder

Speak to the masses, they say
Don't let them forget us
Teach them where they came from
Let them know that they have pride

As I look into the clouds
I see Malcolm, and Martin
Rosa, Harriet, and Sojourner
All who have come before

They infuse in me who I am
What I have become
Everything that I will be
I don't intend to let them down

## **Ghosts**

As I sleep at night I hear the voices
of the ones who have gone before me

We all know about
Martin Luther King, Malcolm X, and Emmitt Till
But what of the names of the people that came before them
Were they not as important? Did not their lives mean as much?

Rev. George Lee was killed
because he urged his people to vote
Lamar Smith was killed
in broad daylight for getting people to vote.

No one would admit that they saw a white man kill a black man
Willie Edwards was forced at gunpoint to jump into a river,
because the Klan thought he was someone else,
he wasn't found for 3 months

Herbert Lee was killed
by a State legislator who was never arrested.
The only witness, a black man was also killed later

The Birmingham 4,
Addie Mae Collins, Denise McNair,
Carole Robertson and Cynthia Wesley.
4 little girls wanting to serve their lord
when they were killed by a cowardly act
Lost in this was the same day death of Virgil Lamar Ware,
a little boy in the wrong place at the wrong time.
His crime; riding his bike.

Women, children, black, and white all killed
while trying to further the cause of equality

These are the people I hear, the ghosts that I see
Their stories are what speak to me

A role call of some of the pioneers that have gone before us. Let us not forget these men, women and children who paved the way for us to enjoy our lives as we know them:

Rev. George Lee
Lamar Smith
Emmett Till
John Earl Reese
Willie Edwards
Herbert Lee
Paul Guihard
Medgar Evers
Addie Mae Collins
Denise McNair
Carole Robertson
Cynthia Wesley
Virgil Lamar Ware
Rev. Bruce Klunder
Rev. James Reeb
Viola Gregg Liuzzo
Dr. Martin Luther King
Malcolm X

## My Name is Emmett

My name is Emmett Till…and I am dead
I was 14 years old when I died in Mississippi
What was my crime, they say I whistled at a woman;
A white woman

I was beaten and shot and thrown in to a river
Even though what I did might have been wrong
I didn't deserve to die, did I?

They say I help start the civil rights movement
I don't know about that, I was just a kid
Medgar Evers and more would come to find out my story
8 years later he would meet the same fate
in the driveway of his home

Why was I killed, no one knows really. For her honor maybe?
That seems to be the thought. To remind us of our place
It didn't remind us of our place
We rose up to take our place in the sun

Martin, Malcolm and the panthers they all fought for our freedom
"I have a dream", "By any means necessary", and "black power"
These were our cries

But it took the murder of a 14 year old child from Chicago, IL
to bring it to the front

My name is Emmett Till…and I died.


**Emmett Till was murdered August 28, 1955.
Let us not forget him and the others
Who died in the struggle!

# A Soldier's Testament

I stand here persecuted
The things they say…refuted
Persecution…don't sing it
Execution…bring it

I am a lyrical assassin
Don't hold back, go all in
Listen now to the worlds that I speak
That you will find the knowledge that you seek

Rejected and disrespected
Our lives unprotected
Chains ingrained
Scars remain

Families ripped apart, torn asunder
Did you think we would fall, just fold under
Our strength comes from queens and kings
Hear our voices, hear us sing

If I must fall, to help my people rise
I give myself, the joy in my demise
For I am not the only one to share in the dream
I am just a member, a part of the team

So do your worst, I welcome the pain
I do this not for fame or gain
I speak for the children, the ones to come
They are our future, they are the ones

So when I'm gone, laid to rest
My life opened, my actions will attest
A soldier I was who fell for the cause
One not subject to archaic laws

I answered to a higher power, one on the side of right
I did my best, I fought the good fight
Stood my ground ornery and contrary
Did what I needed, by any means necessary

# **Reflections of our Ancestors**

I sit back and reflect on the ones that have come before
The things they saw, the pain they had to endure
Marching for our rights, the right to be considered whole
Not 3/5 of a man because of his linage, not to play a role

Beaten, killed, lynched marked with a bulls eye on their back
Subject to anything, random violence, straight out attack
Not only from the Ku Klux Klan, but from the face of the law
Racist, uninformed, indignant, falling into a turbulent maw

Standing tall regardless of the circumstance, hearts on fire
They walked hand and hand, they would not tire
Strength and endurance, they would not stop, could not
The fate of a people they carried, they could not drop

I hear the voices, the whispers in the wind
The ghosts that help me, tell me where to I begin
To tell the stories that must be told
To show the way, to continue to be bold

I reflect on those who have come before me
Who have opened mine eyes so that I could see
Who have spoken so that I may tell
The stories and the pain, our own personal hell.

## **Predator**

I am a predator
I am not your friend
I am knowledge incarnate
Step to me…please

If you disrespect my people
I will find you
If you spread what you do not understand
I will find you

I am the protector of all which is sacred
To my people
I will not stand for that which is
Rude, crude, or socially abstrude

For 400 years we have been put down
Walked upon, frowned upon
Beaten, lynched and forgotten

NO MORE!

I will not stand nor will I tolerate
The bullshyt and the ignorance
That is common place

THIS STOPS NOW!

We must learn to respect ourselves
Because if we don't respect our selves
How can we expect anyone else to?

I cry when I see what we have devolved into
It's as if everything that we fought for
Bled for, died for
No longer matters

I am a predator
I am not your friend
I am knowledge incarnate
Step to me…please

## 4 little girls

It was a Sunday, just like any other Sunday
Songs of praise lifting into the morning sky
4 little girls filling their hearts with joy
Praising their god, loving their lord

Then in a second that all came to an end
From a cowardly act by a few racist men
4 little girls, their lives ended
This act calloused, the damage intended

4 little girls killed by 4 racist men
Their promise ended, no one knows what they could have been
My heart aches to see any life come to an end
But it hurts me now, as it did then

What was in their minds on that fateful day?
How would they know, with their lives they would have to pay?
For a struggle that went on after they were gone
Unwitting soldiers in a battle that had yet to be won

4 little girls, their lives taken away
the violence resonates, even today
Listen carefully as history whispers from the flames
Cherish your children, teach them their names

Addie Mae Collins
Carole Robinson
Cynthia Wesley
Denise McNair

15 September 1963, marked the end of their short life
Empowering the struggle, enhancing the strife
Remembering this, after all these years
4 little girls can invoke emotions and tears

# **7089**

7089. This is your way to identify me now.
Reduced to a number, I don't even rate a name
Less than a man, just 4 digits in a log
You can't deny what I am and what I am scares you

I am not the movement; I am the face of the movement
Remove me and there will be others to take my place
We will continue to make your life a living hell
You have awoken the beast and now it is time to pay

You have beaten, lynched and persecuted my people
We've continued to march for our rights, to sit in for our rights
Use your water hoses and your dogs on my people
We are strong in the fact that we will not back down

200,000 strong heard the speech on the mall in Washington
We all have a dream that will one day come true
Despite all that you try,
one day you will realize that you cannot win
Jim Crow will cease to exist, segregation will cease to exist

7089. A number for a man in a cell. Yet I am not afraid
I am on the side of right and shall prevail
Even thought I may not reach the other side of the mountain
I will be free at last, thank god almighty I will be free at last

## Change

Everybody always wants change
They don't do this, they don't do that
Have you ever thought that,
you can effect change?
Stop complaining, get off your ass!
If our ancestors didn't effect change
We would not be where we are

What if Martin Luther King didn't have a dream?
If Malcolm X didn't preach by any means necessary
What would have happened if
there was no Underground Railroad?
What if Rosa Parks had not given up her seat on the bus?
Where would we be if there was no march on D.C?
Or Selma, or Montgomery, Alabama?

Where would our children be if
the 9 young children didn't integrate the schools in Arkansas?
Where would we be if people like,
Emmett Till, Medgar Evers, and the 4 young girls in Birmingham
hadn't given their lives
Where would we be if
the very thing that they fought for didn't exist?

We take for granted the most powerful tool that we have
The right to vote
Afro Americans have the lowest voter turnout, but yet
we scream the loudest when we think we aren't represented fairly
But for once we rose up an effected change,
his name is Barrack Obama

If you don't like what is going on, do something about it
Let your voice be heard, don't sit back and complain
Be proactive, get out and vote, get the family out to vote

Don't let the blood, sweat and tears have gone by the wayside

Only you can effect change
Be a part of the solution
Not the problem

## <u>Soldier</u>

I am a soldier to the cause
I will fight for what is right
I will do what needs to be done
To the end if need be

I speak for my people
I work for my people
I live and die for my people
I am my people

You come at me with idiosyncrasy
And dated memories
I am not what you think
Strength flows through me

Forget what you heard
It's not real anymore
I am here and I will be heard
No longer will I be disregarded

My people marched, fought and died
Were lynched, jailed, burned
Kidnapped, hung, and shot
No more. No more

I am a soldier
My heart bleeds the cause
I am in this to the end
If you don't believe me

**TRY ME!**

## Footsteps

I walk in the footsteps of greatness
I follow the path of the righteous
for those who have died so that
I may be who I am I thank you.
From Harriet Tubman to Rosa Parks
from Frederick Douglass to Dr Martin Luther King
From Emmett Till to the Birmingham 4
you opened the gate, so I could walk through the door
Stokely Carmichael, The panthers, and Malcolm X
the weight you had to carry
You bared your souls by any means necessary
I will follow in your steps, but not the only one
So let it be written, so let it be done

## **Hatred**

I can see it in your eyes
I can feel it radiate from your soul
Why do you feel it so?
What have we done to deserve this?

Hatred

You teach it to your children
You preach it to your masses
You make it your doctrine
You make it your law

Hatred

You kill, maim, and destroy
and for what
Is it the color of my skin?
Is it what I stand for?

Hatred

Why am I hated so
subjugated, and submissed
Dismissed and unseen
Tried and crucified

Hatred

Let it go, let it disperse
No need to let it fester
because hatred or not
I will survive

# Her Journey

*Grandma, why do you cry when you look at that picture?*

*This picture is of your great-great great grandmother. My mother's mother grandmother and she was a slave.*

*What's a slave grandma?*

*It's a person who has to do something against their will. In this case, they were brought to this land without wanting to be here.*

*Is it a bad thing?*

*Yes baby, come over here and I will tell you what my mother told me...*

It started in a little village in Nigeria. Her name was Abisola which meant "*born into a wealthy family*" and she was the daughter of an Oba or chief. She was an only daughter. She grew up with her Iya learning how to become a woman. She was the apple of her father's eye and he made sure that everything was taken care for her.

In the beginning of her 12<sup>th</sup> season, her father came to her and said that she would be married to the son of another Oba. This would ensure peace between the two tribes. Her Iya said is this a good thing? I have had dreams about this and there can be nothing but bad to be come of this. Her father said things will be okay. It will happen on the son's fourteenth year, which will be in 14 days time.

Little did she know that in 14 days she would never see any of her new or old family again.

Over the next few days her Iya showed her the things that she would need to know to take care of herself and her new husband to be. She explained to her about her time, when mother earth caused her to flow to cleanse herself and that no man was to touch her during that time. How to prepare certain dishes that would insure that she would be fertile. She would be ok, or so she thought.

On the morning of her betrothed 14th season, her Iya dressed her in a ceremonial dress that she had made for her. She looked at her and said you leave here a child, but tonight you will be a woman. She hugged her tightly, not knowing that this would be the last time she would ever see her daughter again.

They traveled to the next village, where she would no longer be a little girl, she would become a woman. I'm scared she told her Iya. So was I. you will learn everything that you need to know. I have taught you everything that my Iya taught me. All will be good.

Soon their party arrived at the tribe of her betrothed. She was put in to a hut of her own, as she was not to see her man until sunset. Her Iya and the Iya of Adebayo attended to her. She was bathed in a bath of milk and honey as befitting a wife of a first born. Her hair was done with flowers placed in it. She was placed in a gown of pure silk and fed dates and drank goat's milk. She was left alone to rest as it would be a long night.

Soon sunset had come and it was time. A ceremonial veil was put over head and she was let out to meet her new husband. A feast was held uniting the two tribes was held and she was introduced to her husband. She was scared when she saw him. She was so small in stature and he was so big. They sat together and began to talk to each other and she began to get more comfortable with him. Maybe this would not bad at all. Finally they went to their hut and began to make love. Her Iya had tried to explain to her the pain of her first time, but she did not expect the searing pain as he entered her. He grunted and he felt her blood flow proving that she was indeed a virgin. He was gentle with her though and soon she began to enjoy herself and gave herself to her husband.

She did not remember falling asleep but she awoke to a great commotion outside of her hut there were strange men fighting with the men of the tribe with these fire sticks she watched her father fall and there was so much blood. She was grabbed by two men and drug into her hut. She screamed *Adebayo! Adebayo!* and then all went dark.

She awoke to men arguing over her. You killed her, one man screamed. She would have brought a fair price. She is not dead; I just hit her hard enough to knock her out. But what about all the blood, I didn't do that it was here when we drug her in here. Her legs were covered with it. My god she's only a child. Well pick her up we need to get going. The men are already gone. What few women there are will go on another ship. We will have to make 3 more stops to pick up the rest of them. She did not say a word. She could not understand them but she had a feeling this was the last time she would see her home land again.

She faded in and out as they traveled through the jungle. Eventually she awoke and found that she was chained to another female as they walked. There were many prayers and wailing as they made their journey. She had no idea as to where they were going but she only know that it was not back to her home.

Every day it seemed that someone died. They took them out of the chains and let them lay to be eaten by the animals of the jungle. She willed herself not to die in the jungle; she was determined to make it to the end.

After six cycles of the sun, they made it to the big water. She thought that she saw Adebayo but she could not yell to him. She had no voice, her voice was parched. She saw in front of her the biggest boat that she had ever seen. She was now truly scared. Her heart began to pound, and her legs began to shake. One of the men dragged her on board and chained her into the bowels of the boat. Now she knew all was lost and finally she began to cry.

For many cycles of the sun she traveled. Some of the women on the boat died from disease and hunger. They were thrown overboard. Once every few days they were washed with sea water, especially during their time with mother earth. The salt in the water burned their wounds from their chains but she did not cry out. She would not give in, she would not submit.

One morning she heard a yell from the deck. We are here, we are here! We can finally get these miserable wenches off this boat. It's bad luck to have a woman on a boat anyway. Get them up here and put those burlap dresses on them. She was brought up to the deck with the rest of the women, and marched to the holding pen. There they were ogled by these pale men and pointed at by their women. There were people of her own color but they would not look at them. One by one they were brought out and looked at. They checked their hair for mites, made sure that they had all their teeth. Some of the men squeezed their breasts and even stuck their fingers inside of them. One man tried that with her and she bit him. He slapped her so hard she saw stars. They removed him away from her and another one took a look at her and said you will come home with me. She didn't understand him but there was something in his voice that made her think that it would be alright.

The man who had slapped her tried to bid on her, but the kind man was able to purchase her. Come with me he said. He took her chain and moved off and she followed, puzzled as to why she was now to leave with him. I need someone young to help keep my house. My slave that I have now is old and will not be able to it for much longer. So you will have to learn and learn quickly. She will teach you everything that you will need to know.

After a ride of one sun's cycle they arrived to his house. As she was the only slave that he had bought , it didn't take long to get her out of the wagon. Jezzy, he called. Jezzy come and see who I have brought to help you. I don't need any help, a soft voice said; I can still do what needs to be done around here. Sure you can old woman, come help get her settled. A woman who reminded her of her Iya walked out and looked at her. She is only a child, why did you buy her? To keep her away from Jones, he said. He felt her up right there and then when she bit him he hit her. I almost killed him then and there. The old woman looked at her and said come on child I'll get you settled.

Over time Jezzy taught her how to read the language and how to read and write. But the older woman was getting weaker. Abi as they called her now began to take over more and more of the day to day work, until one day she was doing everything that needed to be done in the house. The man said nothing but complimented her on the house and dinner from time to time.

One morning Abi went in to give Jezzy her morning coffee but the old woman wouldn't wake up. She ran to get the man and they both ran back to her little house, but it was too late. Jezzy had passed during the night. He came out and said the house is yours now. You will stay here; we will have a service for Jezzy this afternoon. My name is Johnson, Sean Johnson. Don't worry about breakfast today I don't think I could eat. Abi stayed with the old woman until some men came to get her to take her to be buried. Abi prayed that Jezzy would find peace and that what god she believed in would take care of her in the afterlife.

Over the next ten years coming to her 24$^{th}$ season or year, she watched over Mr. Johnson and took care of his house. He had never been married and had received his farm from his parents. He had no need for a large plantation, as he had money, but had a modest farm with 10 slaves that he treated well. He also had a running feud with Jones, his neighbor to the west of him. Jones wanted his land and had staged raids but had not been successful.

Early one fall morning Abi smelled smoke, and ran out of her house to see the big house in flames. She tried to run into the house but an old field hand named jebidiah stopped her. We need to go child, there is nothing we can do for the massa. He was shot in the back by Jones. We need to leave. If we can get to the Underground Railroad, we can get to the north and we can be free. But we have to go now! Abi took a look back and the burning house and said a silent prayer for Sean's soul and ran into the woods.

For the next 3 months Abi's life consisted of running from place to place. Sleeping and hiding during the day, and moving during the night. Jebidiah saved her life one night when they were almost caught by slave hunters. He gave his life so that she could escape.

She made her way to the town of Ripley, Ohio where she was able to start her life over. She got a job in a seamstress shop. It was here that she met her future husband, who was a blacksmith. They were married and had your great-great grandmother. She told her story to her and it has been passed down to the firstborn grandchild every since...

The granddaughter looked up at her and asked, *"Do you think that slavery will return?"*

*No baby that is why we tell these things to you and when you get older, you will do the same.*

*Yes grandma I will, I truly will.*

## <u>My Calling</u>

This is my calling, this is what I do
to raise up the ancestors, bring their stories to you
share their stories, make you feel their pain
raise it up, go against the grain

My calling is to educate, minds to illuminate
rumors to disintegrate, lives to integrate
show the love, to bring them from the past
To tell their stories, put them to the top of the mast

Ah! But you don't hear me though!

Rise up; Stand up drink from the cup
Sit with Martin and Malcolm and take your sup
run with Harriet and Sojourner, freedom at all cost
The Underground Railroad, lives can't be lost

My calling is to enlighten, people to brighten
history to tighten, pride to heighten
youngsters to teach, sometimes I might have to preach
dreams to reach, can you feel me I stick like a leach

Ah but you don't hear me though!

## My Life

*Paw-paw what did you do when you grew up?* My grandson asked me one day.

*When I grew up there were things that I couldn't do. Like what he asked. Well I couldn't go in the front door of a restaurant, had to sit in the back of a bus, things like that.*

He thought for a minute and looked up and said, *that's not right.*

*No it's not, but it happened. Come sit in paw-paw's lap and let me tell you a story. I remember it as if it was yesterday....*

I grew up in the Deep South. Racism was rampant and it was status quo. Colored as we were called then were expected to know our place. Yes suh and no suh were the words that were to be said when speaking to white folk. Our women raised their children and washed clothes and cleaned their homes, while the men worked at what menial jobs there were. There was nothing for a kid in the fifties to do but stay out of the way.

Every so often you would hear about someone being killed or disappearing and not being found. You would see the men in the white sheets and you learned to keep out of the way. You saw the houses being burned and people hung from trees. You would hear of the riots in other cities and wonder if it would ever happen here. No of course not. No one cared what happened here.

Then in 1955 two things happened that changed my outlook on life and the way we lived. In august a 14 year old boy named Emmett Till was kidnapped, beaten and shot. His killers were never convicted. In December, a lady named Miss Rosa Parks refused to give up her site on a city bus. These two things brought a new awareness to the struggle of colored people and the fight for equality.

I sat and watched the things that went on over the next couple of years with the movement. In 1957, even though a federal order was issued, nine children were refused entry into a high school in little rock, Arkansas. Federal troops were needed for them to gain entry.

Over the next few years a non-violent movement called the sit in was the primary tool for the movement. But in the next few years in the sixties they would become bloody for anyone involved.

In 1961, I was riding a greyhound bus along with other protesters of the law saying that that there could be no segregation in interstate travel facilities. As we traveled our bus was stopped by an angry mob and our bus was fire-bombed. By the grace of god no one was killed but things would get a lot worse before it got better

In 1963, the movement was rocked with the loss of Medgar Evers, killed in his own driveway, and the deaths of 4 young girls in the bombing of a church in Birmingham Alabama. This shook us to the core, but it only firmed up our resolve to see this through to the end. We had been beaten, lynched, kidnapped, some never to be seen again. But for everyone that fell, someone else was there to take their place.

The years went by and the struggle continued. We lost Martin and Malcolm. But the original Civil rights act was signed, and executive order 11246 which opened up affirmative action for minorities was put into action. Even though it had been bloody, and costly in terms of life, we had prevailed. But now I'm not so sure...

*Why paw-paw?*

*No one pays attention to the lessons learned from those days. Kids these days think they are entitled to everything, when they are not.*

*Racism is still here. Our people are still losing our lives. It seems no one cares.*

*I do paw-paw, I do. And I will do something when I grow up.*

*I know you will, but I hope that you won't have to. I really do.*


I AM... SOMEBODY! I AM... SOMEBODY!
I AM... SOMEBODY!!!

## Am I Not a Man?

Am I not a man and a brother?
Do I not feel or love?
Do I not care?
Do I not want?

Have I not endured pain?
Have I not bled for you?
Have I walked for you?
Have I not died for you?

Have I not cried for you?
Have I not tried for you?
Have I not prayed for you?
Have I not been betrayed for you?

These things I ask
These things I wish to know
These things I wish to discover
Am I not a man and a brother?

# Rage Against the Machine

I rage against you, you who have held my people down
You have caused my people to transgress, regress
Instead of progress
I rage against the machine

I rage against the mob mentality that you have used against us
Lynching, kidnapping, Jim Crow
3/5 of a man? Are you serious?
I rage against the machine

I rage for those who cannot stand for themselves
Stand up get up. We who can should. We who should will!
No one will give you anything free, take what you need
I rage against the machine

I rage against the machine
We should teach, preach, and inform not conform
Yell, tell, if you can't take it, go to hell!
I rage against the machine

I rage because someone has to
I rage because someone needs to
I rage for my people to be seen
I rage against the machine

## **Revolution**

The revolution shall not be televised
We are tired of your
empty promises
Fake words
Weak action

The revolution shall not be televised
If we have to march …we will
If we have to protest…we will
If we have to riot…we will

The revolution shall not be televised
We are not our ancestors
We are empowered with knowledge
And the ways and means to use it

The revolution shall not be televised
Dogs and fire hoses won't work
Not this time

The revolution shall not be televised
The power of the pen
Freedom of speech
And the right to vote will be your downfall

The revolution shall not be televised
This time it will be you who will have to look over your shoulder;
You who will wonder where the next salvo will be fired from

Beware
We are coming
And you won't know when
Or where because...
The revolution shall not be televised

## Rise

Damn!
I see what you do and it shakes me to the core
Damn!
I'm not taking this bullshyt no more

It's time for all this to come to an end
It's time for all black people to go back to where we began

Raise up, get your mind right
Forget this me and I, we need one sight
We are own worst enemy, we're doing the man's job
Steal from each other, instead of him trying to rob

But you don't hear me though

Get off your ass, get educated
Help your people, stop being in grated
The ancestors didn't do what they did for us to throw it away
Not for the things they did, with their lives they had to pay

Get up get up, fight for your rights
Standing together, we have our collective might
Get up my people; we won't stand for more lies
Get up, rise black people rise!

# Sista's of the Civil Rights Movement

We all know about the men in the civil rights movement
Dr. Martin Luther King, Malcolm X, Medgar Evers to name a few.
But other than Miss Rosa Parks,
were there any women that took a stand?
Were there any others that raised their voices and said,
we will not take this
Anymore, we will not be treated as second class citizens,
we are god's children
And we shall overcome!

Mary McLeod Bethune- creator of schools for black children
and founder of Bethune-Cookman College.

Linda Brown- while even though just a third grader was
instrumental in the integration of
elementary schools in Topeka, Kansas.

Ruby Bridges- The first black student at
her elementary school in New Orleans
She endured death threats and violence,
all in the pursuit of a decent education

Sojourner Truth- one of the first to speak out about slavery.
She was also the first to win a lawsuit against
white people to win custody of her son

Dorothy Cotton-as the education director for the SCLC,
helped the 1963 Birmingham movement

The list goes on.
And I would be remiss if I didn't mention,
Mrs. Coretta Scott King, who
took over her husband's work after he died.

A salute to the women, black and white,
who shed blood, sweat, and tears, to advance of
the Afro-American during those turbulent times.
And to those who gave their lives, we are eternally grateful.

## <u>Sit In</u>

You tell me that I can't sit here
Why is that? Please explain
Aren't we made in god's own image?
What makes you better than me?

Is it because my skin is dark?
Is it because my hair is nappy?
I have money, I can pay
What makes you better than me?

Why do I have to come in the back door?
Sit in a corner, or take my food out back
Drink from a different water fountain
What makes you better than me?

Why must I go to sub-standard schools?
Or sit in the back of the bus
Why must I walk in fear of my life?
What makes you better than me?

Why must I find a cross burning in my yard
See pictures of my people strung up
People killed just for the color of their skin
What makes you better than me?

I sit here because I can, because I must
I'm tired of being thought as second rate
But once again I would really like to know
What makes you better than me?

## <u>Strength</u>

I feel if I have the weight of the world on my shoulders
I carry the hopes and dreams of my people
I speak so that we may all be heard
My strength and faith is all that I have

I raise mine self to the almighty and pray
That he will give me the strength to last
To endure the pain and the hatred
To take those that would take me away

I speak to the masses to restore our pride
And yet I am ignored, passed by
We no longer wish to improve our lot
Status quo has become the norm

We are the descendants of the kings and queens of Africa
Royal blood flows through our veins
Yet we are reduced to walking with our pants around our azz
And our women letting themselves be prostituted for gain

NO! Again I say NO! It pains me to see what we have become
Our children have no clue from where we come
Our history has be convoluted, diluted
Our leaders forgotten, down trodden

We have been reduced from a mighty people
To a footnote, left to be celebrated one a year
We who had the strength to endure
kidnapping from our motherland
Now are a joke, a laughing stock, and the blame of all evil

We are our own worst enemy, instead of helping one another
We think of ways to bring them down and to discredit
Petty jealousy, greed, and envy

We are no better than those who have made it their life's work

I ask my creator for the strength to hold up my people
To continue to speak on their behalf
To show them the way
To shoulder our pride, our history, who we are

## Step To Me If You Dare

Step to me if you dare
I am not one to be trifled with
I am a black man unleashed
Step to me you will need a priest

I am your worst nightmare
A man with knowledge and the know how to use it
I have a long memory and I don't forget
The things done to my people, we not finished yet

For too long we have had to deal with your kind
No longer I say it's time to have a new frame of mind
Study long, study wrong, I think you've sealed your deal
Rage not compassion is the thing I feel

The bible says,
*"do unto others as you would have them do unto you"*
Did you miss this part,
or does this not pertain to the things that you do
Remember these words, no more compromising
You have been witness to a black man rising!

# The Whisper

Can you hear it? The whisper
The voices of the past
The echoes of our ancestors

Can you hear Sojourner Truth?
And Harriet Tubman
Come with me to be free

Can you hear the screams of Emmett Till?
And the 4 little girls in Birmingham
Lives ended before their time

Did you hear the joyful noise of the freedom riders?
As they sang "we shall overcome"
Even as they were arrested and taken away

Did you hear Dr King as he spoke upon the mall?
"Free at last! Free at last! Thank God Almighty,
we are free at last!"

Can you hear Brother Malcolm telling our people?
To protect themselves *by any means necessary*

The voices of those who came before continue to speak to us
They whisper in the wind
All you have to do is

Listen.....

# Time Traveler

I feel myself moving, flowing through time
One second I am walking with chains, trapped as a slave
The next I walk on Wall Street with suit and tie
Still just as trapped, a different type of slave

I'm running with Harriet Tubman,
down the Underground Railroad
Running to be free
I see Tommie Smith and John Carlos
standing with their hands held high
Still running for freedom,
in a different place and time

I'm standing in Birmingham
at the church where the little girls would die
Knowing what I know the tears come to my eye
I stand in Memphis waiting for the final shot to come it seems
I yell but no one can hear me, they have silenced Dr King's dream

I see these things in our history,
to repeat them to my fill
I tried but could not stop the murder of Emmitt Till
I marched in Selma, Washington, and Birmingham
I watched the riots in LA when Rodney king was slammed

I watched my people, bloody, battered and torn
I watched them persevere and a new day was born
It's time to move on; you will hear my echoes in your mind
I feel myself moving, flowing through time

## **<u>Walk</u>**

I walk through the land of righteousness
I see the meanings of the past
I feel the pain and anguish of our people
I hurt along with those who have gone on

I walk down the streets of Selma, Alabama
Marching for our rights
Attacked because of our skin
Ridiculed because of our faith and strength

I walk past the church where the four little ones died
I feel the pain and the horror of the people around them
I see the little boy who died by the same hand
In the wrong place at the wrong time

I walk through Mississippi, where a young boy was killed
For whistling at a woman of a different color
Beaten, shot and thrown into a river
A life gone too soon

I walk in Washington DC in the march on the capital
A place where a dream took shape
Yet I walked past the hotel in Memphis
Where they tried to silence that same dream

Once again I walked to DC in modern times
When Black men, a million men strong
Announced we are still here, we still have a dream
We will not go quietly into the night

I walk in the hoods, and my heart falls
My children killing themselves
Not knowing from whence they came
And most of all not caring

I walk in Texas, watching a black man dragged to his death
Seeing another run down in a parking lot
And for what... Sport?
Because someone said lets go kill us a nigger
Why does this still exist?

I walk into my home town and look at the wall of the courthouse
And gaze upon the words colored and white
Painted over for years and years
But still able to be seen

I walk wondering what will happen to my people
Will we survive? Who will step forth? Who will care?
Who is willing to step into the shoes?
Who will walk along with me?

## Who

I wonder who will teach our children
Not about reading, writing, or arithmetic
Who will teach them about us?
Who will teach them about our people?

Who will teach them that they descend from kings and queens?
That even while being taken from their homes they persevered
Kept trying to gain their freedom even when they knew
That it might cost them their life

Who will tell them about Harriet Tubman and Sojourner Truth?
Strong black women, first in a line that continues today?
Marian Anderson, Lena Horne, Mary McLeod Bethune
Condi Rice, Mae Jemison, and Miss Rosa Parks.

Who will tell them about the brothers
that carried us on their backs?
During the dark times when we were considered less than human
Malcolm X, Martin Luther King,
Stokely Carmichael, Medgar Evers
Dr George lee, and many more

Who will explain about the marches on
Washington D.C and Selma, Alabama?
Who will talk about the freedom riders,
and the sit-ins and the protests?
Who will show the pictures of brothers and sisters attacked?
Arrested, beaten and killed

Who will explain to them about the children who gave their lives?
About Emmett till, the 4 little girls in Birmingham
But also the 9 brave children who integrated the schools in
Arkansas

Who will show them that they can achieve
anything that they want to do
Even when they are told they can't
The Tuskegee airmen,
George Washington carver, George Alcorn,
Madame C.J. Walker, Dr Daniel Williams

Who will show them that racism is still alive and well?
Tell them about the cross burnings that continue to this day
Show them that we still lose our lives
The two men in Texas come to mind

Who will teach them that they have to learn?
So that they can pass it on to their children
And their children's children…

**I will…I will**

## **Would You?**

Would you give your life for what you believed in?
Would you let yourself be beaten? Jailed?
Our ancestors did.
They felt so strongly that they did what was necessary
Sometimes they paid with their lives

Would you march knowing that you may be spit upon?
Kicked, shot with water hoses, had dogs sicced upon you?
They did. By force of will because
they knew their purpose was just
They knew that they had to prevail

Would you live in a time where
you knew you were marked for death?
Because of the color of your skin. Just because you existed.
That you may die because you looked at someone the wrong way
Or because you may have spoken
without the right humility in your voice

Would you have spoken out against
injustice knowing you might die?
Would you walk on the front line knowing
the bull's-eye was centered on your chest?
Would you lead others knowing that you
might not be there to see the end result?
Brothers Malcolm and Martin did,
because our people needed leaders

These things I ask because our people need leaders more than ever
Racism has reared its head now more than ever
Our people are still being killed
for no more that the color of their skin
We fight each other instead of the system

I will do what I can to help our people keep their place
I have seen what has transpired,
people killed, crosses burned
I know what I would do to help us along.

The question is...

**Would you?**

## <u>Walking</u>

It is March 7, 1965 and we stand waiting
600 strong black and white
We shall take our cause from
Selma to Montgomery, in this bastion of racism

Alabama

We begin to walk arm in arm

ATTACKED!

Tear gas! Billy clubs!
Run back to Selma
Battle lost, but not the war
We shall overcome

We come back
5 times as many
3200 strong
We will preserve

On March 25, we arrived
Our grievances redressed
The president saw things our way
The voting rights passed because of this day

I'm old and gray now
Can't walk quite as far
But I remember it all
And would do it again

Young people get your life together
It's not about what you have
What you can get
Things are not always what they seem

Help each other, fight for each other
Love each other
You are the future of our people
What legacy will you leave?

## <u>Who Are You?</u>

Who are you? Where do you come from?
I know who I am and from whence I came
I am descended from kings and pharaohs
Royal blood flows through my veins

I am the epitome of your worst nightmare
A strong black man regal beyond compare
I fear you not; there is nothing you can do
My heart is pure, my soul is true

I am the voice of my people, strong and proud
You will hear me coming, my voice loud
I will stand against you, even if it means my life
I will not retreat; I will not bow to your strife

Look over your shoulder, for things are about to change
We are tired of the bullshyt, the revolution is in range
I intend to teach, preach and empower
Yell, tell and enlighten. Minute by minute, hour by hour

Woman to woman, man to man, this is our call
Together we stand, divided we will fall
I stand at the front of the line, my pride ever shining
I am who I am

A BLACK MAN RISING!

## Nubian Man

Nubian man where are you, where u be
Brought here to this place against your will
Shackled and chained
Herded like oxen. placed in a cage

Nubian man how do you survive
In this land far away from home
From a family you will never see
In a country far away

Nubian man whipped beaten castrated
Marked with a brand like cattle
Disrespected, learn a new language
You're not whole, given another name

Nubian man run if you can, get away
Run, run from the dogs and the hunters
If caught your dead, but maybe not
But you might wish you were when they're through

Nubian man beaten blooded bowed
100 lashes maybe you live maybe not
Example to be made, you are it
No one helps, they look away

Nubian man where are you, where u be
Brought here to this place against your will
You're not who you were, who you used to be
You're just a slave, someone named Toby

## Nubian Woman

Nubian woman where are you, where you be
Strong and lovely there to support your king
Queen beyond compare, strength for the masses
Our help, our wisdom, our love

Nubian woman, neglected by our brothers
Disrespected, abused, misused
Set aside, blacked-eyed
No love shone.

Nubian woman, woman hood taken
Slave masters removed dignity
Pickaninnies born
No love no peace

My sisters fought all their lives
No recognition, no compassion
I am a woman hear me roar
Silence abounds

Masters of the Underground Railroad
Set my people free
Harriet and Sojourner T.
Our women understood what it meant to be free

Nubian women, azz out breast shown
Is this what you are what you have become
Your ancestors cry at the sight
Their queens, the future

Nubian woman where are you, where you be
Strong and lovely there to support your king
No matter what ever problem we may have
You still be a queen to me

## Sight Beyond Sight

I see things sometimes that I don't understand
Things that may or may not happen
Things from the past
People, things, places I never been

Walking into Selma Alabama with Dr King
Standing in the auditorium with Malcolm X
Walking into the school in Little Rock Arkansas
Standing on the mall in Washington DC

Sometimes I wonder why I see what I do
Why I have been chosen to tell and retell the tales
To bring forth the stories of those who have gone before
To bring forth the stories to the light

The things I see shake me to the core
I see what they see, feel what they feel
The lash of the whip, the strike of the cane
Sometimes even the feel of the rope around my neck

I do what I can to teach, to preach
To educate, and illuminate
To tell, even sometimes yell
To bring it forward, so that in your mind it will jell

This thing I do, this challenge I must accept
This pain I feel, for my ancestors I have wept
To try to inform, to make things right
To share what I see, sight beyond sight

# **I Watch**

I've watched
I see all, I know all
I have watched you for ages
I have watched you grow
I have watched you fall

I watched you as you were taken from
Your ancestral homes in chains
Betrayed by your own kind

I watched as you were loaded like
Animals and taken across the vast
Sea to a place that you and your descendants
Would have to make your own

I watched as you were made to be second class citizens
Told that you were not even a whole man
Separated from loved ones, beaten and killed

I watched as you took the Underground Railroad
And found your way to freedom
To make new lives in the north
And grieve for those left behind

I watched those who fell by the wayside
Martin Luther King, Malcolm X, Emmett Till
Medger Evers, the Birmingham 4, and
Those not so well known

I watched the cities burn, the riots attack
The dogs sicced, the water hoses flow
The crosses burned, the cries of those interned

I watched the March on the mall,
and Selma to Montgomery
and little known ones like in Seattle

I watched you rise up to become who you are.

I watched on January 20, 2009
as a man of color became the president
And although we are only to watch, my heart swelled
The people that I had watched over years
Had taken their rightful place

I've watched
I see all
And I will continue to watch
Until the end of time

# Untitled

Where do I begin?
Where do I start?
Where are the answers
to the questions that I must pose?

I walk through life baffled and confused.
Land of the free, home of the brave?
I think not!
The more things change, the more they stay the same.

What kind of world is it when the rich get richer;
The poor get poorer; Robbing Peter to pay Paul?
When a mother shoots her kids and then herself
because she can't get food stamps?

When the homeless walk the streets like zombies
Some by no fault of their own
But you have perfectly good individual begging
Because their too lazy to go and get a job

When the military is used just as a heavy handed bully
When he who has the most toys wins
But when they come home, broken and misused
We tell them thank you, don't let the door knob hit you

When kids don't know how to socialize face to face
It's LOL, OMG, and LMAO
No one plays anymore
Because the schools have ruled that play is too dangerous

Speaking of schools, do they teach anything anymore?
The teachers have sex with children, go on strike
What happened to teaching for the love of the kids?
What happened to no child left behind?

You may look at this as a rant by a bitter old man
But I am concerned about us, not just blacks
Not just whites, all of us, the human race
Soon there will be no race

## The Phoenix

My life is not unlike that of the phoenix
I arise from the ashes of racism
From the dregs of discrimination
I fly with determination

My soul is alight with the strength of my ancestors
Let me get up, stand up, and climb up and over
the mountains of despair, cross the valley of woe
Nothing and no one will hold me down

I soar along the winds of change
Carried aloft with the power of love
My life is in flux, it is never the same
I do what I must to keep myself sane

I am the protector of all that is good
I watch over my people, our history
I am the flame that burns brightly in the night
I am the beacon to bring you home

Even though my time here is short
I will never leave you here alone
I will arise from the bog of hatred
Burning brighter than before

# About The Author

**Anthony Arnold**

A budding Poet and Writer, as early as the third grade when he composed his very first poem, Florida raised writer Anthony Arnold fell in love with words finding them to be a comfort and mainstay throughout his life. Raised to be a reader by his Grandmother, he soon developed a keen awareness and love for Black History. He has a particular gift in this genre although he is one of the most versatile Poets of his generation.

As an avid reader of all genres of literature, he has found a particular passion for Black History. He believes his ancestry and the legacy of those who came before him, gave their blood, sweat and tears to make it possible for him to live a life of freedom and liberation. He is saddened by the fact that it appears the current generation has little knowledge of and doesn't seem to know or speak of Family History, especially Black History. He hopes through his writing he is able to educate others more about the historical significance of the challenges African Americans as well as the contribution of African Americans throughout history including those events which are very rarely discussed or taught in public schools, such as African American roles in the Civil War. He hopes to shed more light on the strength of Black People throughout history.

Although his writing passion is focused a great deal on his own African American Culture Anthony Arnold has a deep love for all mankind that grew during his service to his country. Anthony Arnold has proudly retired from service in the US Air Force. During his career he was awarded numerous medals, including Air Force Achievement Medal-1986, 1993 and 2001 and many more.

This book is the beginning to fulfill his desire to share with the younger generation to inspire them to learn more about their ancestors and culture, letting them know they are much more than what some in society has labeled them.

Anthony is a humble man that uses poetry to express what he knows, believes and passionately feels about culture and history. He appreciates everyone who has come along on his poetic journey of *My People, Our Trials And Tribulations*.

===========

To enjoy more of his poetry please visit his Facebook fan page here

www.facebook.com/AATheTigersDen

*Expressions*

The Voice of the People, Stellar Poet Anthony Arnold writes what others are afraid to. His magnitude stems from activist, teacher, orator and romantic. History will never be silenced. His inspirational and emotional inking educates the reader. You cannot help but feel the story-telling or the poem ignite through his pen. His knowledge illuminates peace and equality universally.
His pen screams for FREEDOM.
His pen screams Individuality.
His pen screams Love.

*Rosemarie Howard*
------------

I remember first reading Anthony Arnold's work and realizing this was a man with a vision...I have watch your work grow over the years and I am honored to say that I know you and honored to follow you on your quest to become the best. Whether the subject is Love, Political, or whatever task you decide to take on He does it well and His work is Flawless...I look forward to being able to purchase a copy of this new book and I wish Him much success and blessings...A True Elite in my book....

*Kenneth McKnight*
------------

Mr. **Anthony Arnold** is the new era to the Power of a Man mind. For each word that you read makes you to want to read even more. I have followed his words and yes I understand his logic and to say this in a positive way... Genius Outstanding Excellence. I can say that once you put your hands on his book you shall want more. Blessing when he allowed us as Poets as Friends to be able to read the Bleed of his INK~! Honor and respect to a good man. The one and only Mr. Anthony Arnold~!

*Rosalind Cherry*

IN LIFE...Sometimes true talent sneaks up on you, from nowhere, with absolutely no warning, and when you are blessed to witness the gift given, the experience is at once exhilarating and simultaneously a breath of fresh air. It is with much anticipation and fanfare that I eagerly await the arrival of the first novel from Anthony Arnold. America and the entire world is about to discern what those in the know have been whispering for years, that this true living legend is the second coming of incredible Authors of yesteryear, from the historic, W.E.B. Dubois, Langston Hughes, and James Baldwin, to current greats such as Walter Mosley. Anthony's considerable skill is matched only by his considerable will in delivering his message to the masses, and I guarantee you will be pleasantly surprised at the result. To read one of his works of art is not to so much read over lines on a page but to actually experience the emotion that oozes from said page as his writs grab you with clever colloquialism's and just plain old down home sobriquets, Anthony invites you to the literary feast of imagination, imbibes you until you are sated, and then refuses to let you leave until you have tasted the sweetest of desserts. With that said America, it is my distinct honor, and pleasure to witness the dreams of a father, a veteran, and a true American hero both in the concise definition and in the abstract world of possibilities. Good Luck, and God speed Anthony Arnold, may you always be blessed with the wind at your back.

*Kevin Bigham*
------------

I must say Anthony is the Oracle of poetry. His ink is stellar and leaves you desiring, questioning, and virtually in anticipation as to what is next in his ink. His essence of self from his soul oozes riches, humbleness, and a deep look into history. Though, I may not have known Anthony for a long period of time, he has captivated me as a writer and as a poet. The world needs to know his pen, and be touched from within, as I have been. It is my honor to be in the presence of GREATNESS!!!!!!

*Latrice Watkins*

During my days of writing poetry has truly been a tremendous blessing granted from my higher father, through my travels in the poetry world I have met many candid writers and people overall. Today I want to give praise and love to one of the most: premiere, awesome, educational grounded; overall a very insightful enlightened writers who voice the fruits of life into words. Mr. Anthony Arnold is what poetry is all about, his words have reached and touched many people and I'm glad to say I'm one of many he has touched through his artistry craft when it comes to poetry. Brother this moment is an honor to me, and even a bigger honor for you; just for this fact your are reaching your goals and through your travels and success you as well have reached and uplifted others, Thank you and may the higher power bless this project.

*Rodney Tyson*
------------

Anthony, you are one courageous extraordinary man. The Day we networked you shared with me.....the gift of love, peace, happiness, and the true meaning on how to stand tall, believing in what to feel, and Knowing yourself worth....You Know like they say...When God Made You Broke the Mold. He only made 1 Anthony Arnold. You are the Joy, the inner soul to everyone's heart. I Love your ink. As I read your words I often see and feel my own heart, and spirit flowing from the page. For every word that you place on your paper. You place it all with Love, keep coming with your words, and Love...For every line that you write...I will continue to read, and post my comments...
My Brother you bring life to everything you write, and I want to Thank you for sharing it all with me...* you are My King, My Brother, and I salute, and raise my hand to Anthony Arnold*
Thank you! Thank you! Thank you!

(Peace Love, and Blessing's)
*Lora Faison*
------------

Words themselves seem to be inadequate in the expounding on

your use of them...Prophetic...introspective...socially and historically aware with an informative edge...I have yet to see a topic... theme...or plot that you could not enhance with your command of textual expression....I am honored and blessed to be your friend....and fan

*Wingman Gerald Green*

------------

Mr. Arnolds work is so pleasurable to read. Although his words hold weight, his poetic pieces never have to be deciphered or decoded. Mr. Arnold's impeccable skill for story telling is masterful as he provides nourishment for the reader's soul. I enjoy his work and recommend his heart felt material

*BlaqueRose poetry*

------------

What can one say about this poet other than the fact that he's excellent and a phenomenal talent. Anthony has for quite some time been quietly perfecting his craft and building a fan base that honors his talents. This artist brings outstanding articulation, balance and a glaring voice to the poetic world and is well loved be many of his friends and fans alike. I and many others have fallen in love with Anthony's level of consciousness, his pen and his heart; a modern man well aware of the "bigger picture" and knows his place and part in the world we live. Truly Anthony is a voice that demands to be heard and his strength and character will carry him to the next level in the world of poetry.

*Jon ThElitepoet Crenshaw*

------------

Compelling, Provocative, Enticing, and Influential are just a few of the words that come to mind when I must consider the versatility and delight of the pen of Anthony Arnold. He soars to new levels each time as he writes from the heart, sincere and poignant. I am honored to be among his peers and highly anticipate great success from this and each subsequent publication. Turn the page; take the journey...and you too will feel the power of his pen.

Cheryl D. Faison
*Sublime Poetess*

------------

I'm so very proud of you big bro...I knew when I begin to read your stories and poems...This man can ink and needs to write a book.
Keep up the good work and let me know whatever I can do to help...I can't wait to get your book. I know when I got my book published it was a feeling you will never forget... you have earned your spot my dear brother... You ink from the heart... well done... Dr. King and all the rest would be proud of you too.

Your sis,
*Author LynnieRose*

------------

Anthony Arnold is my friend. He is a wonderful writer ... I've been reading his work for about a year now, and he has a beautiful pen. The way he writes will blow your mind. He takes his readers on a ride of their life with his creative flow. He can write on any subject. I enjoy reading his work and so do many others .Anyone that get a taste of his work will be hocked for life ...I am and forever will one of his lifelong fans. Blessings Anthony and good luck *hugs*

*Rosilia A. Albert AKA RoseApple/Apples*

------------

Anthony Arnold is one of today's most expressive poets. Unbound in his style as well as genera, he writes about whatever inspires him. His poetry and prose comes at us with a voice that is strong, unwavering, and proud. His ability to reach into the guts of life, and present our humanity to us in a way that is both shocking and still somehow comforting is truly something to experience. He is an honest poet that makes no excuses for pride or shortcomings, rather, his words are a human mirror that shows us how things have been, how they are now, where they are going and teaches us, that like his words...we too have the power to change the world! There is not one person who won't find themselves somewhere within these pages and take something very personal away with them from the experience.

*Nyla Alisia:* Award winning poet and founder of The Speakeasy Cafe Poetry Radio Network